WORLD'S FAVORITE

Intermediate
Violin Pieces

INTERMEZZO
ZIGEUNERWEISEN
MEDITATION

RUMANIAN RHAPSODY
INTERMEZZO
VALSE BLUETTE

AVE MARIA
SERENADE
CZARDAS

DRDLA
DRIGO
FIOCCO

ASHLEY
PUBLICATIONS
Distributed by
Hal Leonard Corporation
and
Music Sales Corporation

KHACHATURIAN
SARASATE
BOCCHERINI

A WORD FROM THE PUBLISHERS

With these two volumes (Worlds Favorite Series Numbers 91 and 92) we are proud to publish a fine new collection of the very best concert pieces for violin and piano: this volume of intermediate and a few more difficult pieces, and the other volume devoted to the easier classics, romantics, and moderns. Our easier volume includes some of the finest pieces chosen from the world famous Century Catalog, never before published in a collection, as well as "The Sting", and the only available arrangement that has all three parts of "Fascination".

The present volume contains Enesco's Rumanian Rhapsody, the Khachaturian "Sabre Dance", Zigeunerweisen, Drigo's Serenade, and the Czardas by Kail , which should become a modern light classic.

Alexander Shealy

Alexander Shealy
Ashley Publications, Inc.

CONTENTS
arranged alphabetically by composer

WORLD'S FAVORITE

Intermediate
Violin Pieces

CONTENTS

ZIGEUNERWEISEN

de SARASATE

SERENADE

DRDLA

WALTZ
from "The Sleeping Beauty"

P. TSCHAIKOWSKY
Arranged by Maurice Lee

MINUET

BOCCHERINI

D.C. al Fine.

SERENADE

R. DRIGO

HUNGARIAN DANCE No. 5

J. BRAHMS
arr. by Calvin Grooms

NOCTURNE in Db

FR. CHOPIN, Op. 27, No.2
Arranged by Calvin Grooms

VALSE BLUETTE

(Air de Ballet)

By R. DRIGO
Arr. by F. Carl Jahn

SANTA LUCIA

TRADITIONAL
Transcribed by
CALVIN GROOMS

POET AND PEASANT

(DICHTER UND BAUER)

Overture

FRANZ von SUPPÉ
Arr. by F. Carl Jahn

WALTZING DOLL

E. POLDINI
Arranged by Calvin Grooms

TWO GUITARS

TRADITIONAL

Transcribed and Arranged by
CALVIN GROOMS

IL TROVATORE

VERDI
Arranged by
SEP. WINNER.

Anvil Chorus.

Allegretto.

HUNGARIAN DANCE No.6

JOHANNES BRAHMS

NOCTURNE (G Minor)

F. CHOPIN, Op. 37, № 1.   SCHUBERT

SERENADE
(STAENDCHEN)

SCHUBERT

FLOWER SONG

GUSTAVE LANGE

AVE MARIA

F. SCHUBERT

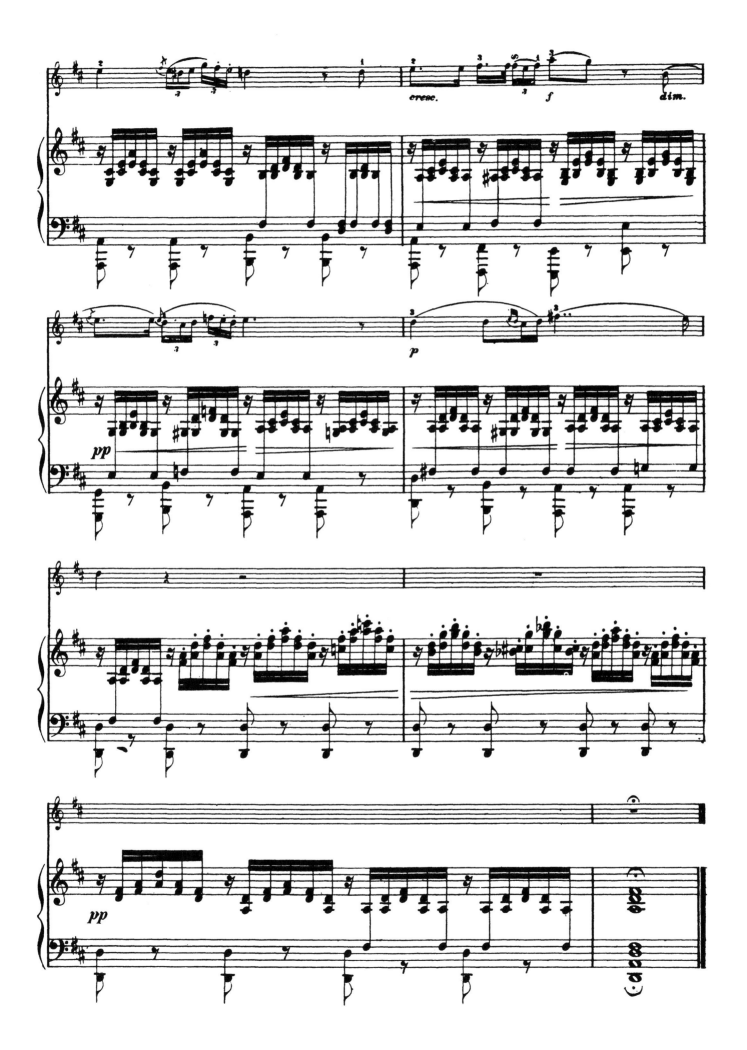

ALLEGRO

GIOSEFFO HECTORE FIOCCO

*) ~ = 𝄽𝅘𝅥 throughout

INTERMEZZO

Souvenir de Vienne

RUMANIAN RHAPSODY

Traditional
ENESCO - KAIL

con tallone

Fine

Fine

Dal Segno con la repetizione e poi Fine

SABRE DANCE

ARAM KHACHATURIAN
Arranged by R. Kail

TANGO

ALBENIZ

MEDITATION

from "Thais"

J. MASSENET

Più mosso agitato

CZARDAS

KAIL

ON WINGS OF SONG

F. MENDELSSOHN

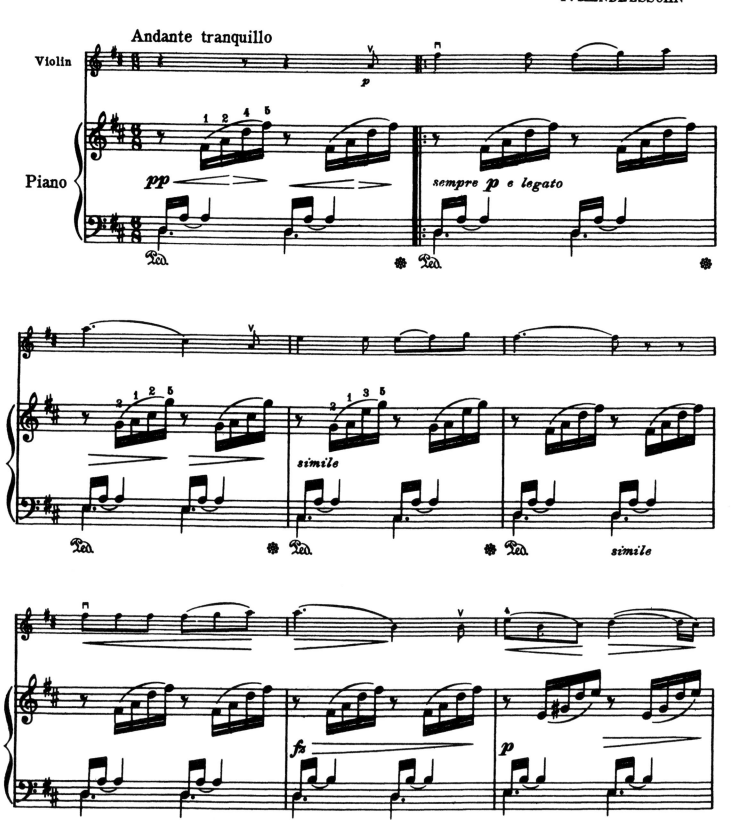

BERCEUSE
from"Jocelyn."

GODARD